Set design by Wilson Chin

Photo by Sandra Coudert

Elizabeth Marvel and Justin Chatwin in the Rattlestick Playwrights Theatre production of *Dark Matters*.

DARK MATTERS

BY ROBERTO AGUIRRE-SACASA

★

★

DRAMATISTS
PLAY SERVICE
INC.

SPECIAL NOTE

DARK MATTERS received its world premiere at Rattlestick Playwrights Theatre (David Van Asselt, Artistic Director; Sandra Coudert, Managing Director) in New York City, opening on November 25, 2006. It was directed by Trip Cullman; the scenic design was by Wilson Chin; the costume design was by Katherine Roth; the lighting design was by Matt Richards; the sound design was by Shane Rettig; original music was composed by Michael Friedman; and the production stage manager was Emily Ellen Roberts. The cast, in alphabetical order, was as follows:

MICHAEL CLEARY .... Reed Birney
JEREMY CLEARY .... Justin Chatwin
SHERIFF BENJAMIN EGAN .... Michael Cullen
BRIDGET CLEARY .... Elizabeth Marvel

CHARACTERS
(in order of appearance)

MICHAEL CLEARY, forties, a novelist
BENJAMIN EGAN, forties, a sheriff
JEREMY CLEARY, sixteen, MICHAEL's son
BRIDGET CLEARY, thirties, MICHAEL's wife

PLACE

Green Bank, Virginia. A small town in the mountains. The Cleary living room. A couch, some chairs, a breakfast table, stairs leading to the bedrooms on the second floor, a front door, a big picture window with a clear view of the outside world.

In the sky, when it's night, lots and lots of stars.

TIME

The present. A week in late fall.

DARK MATTERS

ACT ONE

Darkness. A slow spot comes up on Jeremy Cleary — a sixteen-year-old kid — who talks to the audience.

JEREMY. It's an autumn night, I'm out with my friends, there's a dry, cool breeze blowing down from the mountains, brushing across my face like a ... Rustling through my hair like ... *(Beat.)* Not far from where I am, there's a car sitting on the side of the road, its doors open, light from the dashboard spilling out into the darkness, banishing it ... *(Beat.)* Also close by, but in the opposite direction, there's a house, in the woods, with two people in it, listening to a voice with no body — *(The spot on Jeremy goes out suddenly — he exits — as we hear the beep of an answering machine and the following message:)*
BRIDGET'S VOICE. *(On the machine.)* Hey, guys, it's me, it's Mom. I'm driving, I'm on my way home, I'm stopping to pick up some carrots, some Tropicana, so I'm running behind ... In case you get home, Jeremy, and I'm not there. *(Quick beat.)* And, you know, by all means, feel free to work on the attic. Not my things, just yours ... All right, I'm going now, I love you. *(Another beep! The rest of the lights come up. Michael Cleary, in his early forties, is standing in his living room with another man, who is wearing a sheriff's uniform: Benjamin Egan. They've just listened to Bridget's message on the answering machine.)*
EGAN. The attic?
MICHAEL. Yeah, we're trying to clean it out, we're trying to — It's storage right now, and my wife uses it for an office, but we want to rent it out. It's an ongoing project, cleaning it, and —
EGAN. How long has your wife been missing, Mr. Cleary? *(Short*

pause. Maybe Michael sits on his sofa.)

MICHAEL. You think she's — She *is* missing, then? You think she's — ?

EGAN. How long ago was this message left? Did she leave it — ?

MICHAEL. This afternoon at four o'clock? At the latest, five?

EGAN. The machine says two messages. Was the other from — ?

MICHAEL. Oh, it's just — My — Here, let me — *(Michael hits a button on the answering machine. It beeps and we hear:)*

JEREMY'S VOICE. *(On the machine.)* Hi, Mom, hi, Dad —

MICHAEL. *(Overlapping.)* It's my son — our son — Jeremy, saying he's going out with some —

JEREMY'S VOICE. — I meant, I forgot to tell you, but I'm not gonna be home until, like, I don't know, I'll be back at, like, I dunno, maybe like … twelve? Or so? If it's cool? Twelve? Or one? *(Michael stops the machine.)*

EGAN. He left that at what time?

MICHAEL. After five, sometime after —

EGAN. It's almost one in the morning now, is he — ?

MICHAEL. Still out. *(Beat.)* He doesn't know yet about his — He doesn't know anything yet.

EGAN. And your wife, Mr. Cleary, she's the librarian — ?

MICHAEL. Yes, right, at the —

EGAN. — at the elementary school, yes.

MICHAEL. She called me at three, right when she got off work, to ask if I needed anything from the store, the supermarket, she was going to pick up a few things —

EGAN. Where were you?

MICHAEL. I was at work. She called me on my cell phone.

EGAN. You deliver milk, is that right? That truck out back, in the driveway, that's your milk truck?

MICHAEL. Yes.

EGAN. All right, and is this — would you say this was usual behavior for wife, Mr. Cleary? *(Short pause.)*

MICHAEL. What do you — ?

EGAN. I mean: Has she ever run away — gone missing? Before. *(Short pause.)*

MICHAEL. Yes.

EGAN. She has?

MICHAEL. Since we moved here, yes. She's a — an amateur astronomer, a backyard astronomer. She likes being outside, at

6

night, and sometimes she just — she goes. Without any — Or necessarily telling me, or anyone, where she's going. Until she gets back. From her drives. She takes the car and just — she goes. Up into the mountains to look at the, I don't know, whatever's up there. The stars, the moon, the sky.

EGAN. Okay, this is good news. She's done this before, this is normal behavior —

MICHAEL. Not normal, no, I never said —

EGAN. *Usual* behavior, then, *common* behavior.

MICHAEL. Except — It's always at night — when she goes. This was during the day. She was — interrupted. Her shopping was —

EGAN. How often does she go? At night.

MICHAEL. Two or three times a week, it depends on the weather. I wake up sometimes, in the night, and the house is cold because the front door's open, letting the air in. She just goes out the front door, in her pajamas, and gets into the car and starts driving.

EGAN. But today, in this case: You think she left work, went to the supermarket, came here —

MICHAEL. No, I don't think she — I checked in the refrigerator, but there wasn't anything new. Groceries. That I could tell. But … maybe she did come here and then go, I don't know.

EGAN. She shop the Farmers' Market?

MICHAEL. Yes.

EGAN. I'll head there next. The owner, Victor Billings, is a friend, I can wake him. I've got a picture of your wife, I've got the make of her car — *(He starts out.)*

MICHAEL. How serious is this? How — dire?

EGAN. It's just past one in the morning. Your wife left that message at let's say five. You haven't seen her or heard from her in … that's eight hours. Even with what you've told me about your wife, about her drives … *(The sound of someone fiddling with the front door. Michael and Egan turn to it.)*

MICHAEL. Bridge … *(The front door swings open. Jeremy is standing there, not quite in his right head.)*

JEREMY. Dad, hi — did you get my message? Sorry I'm late, but I was with some friends, and we were on the mountain, looking up at the sky and there were all these strange — all these *crazy* — lights and colors. Like the Aurora Borealis, but *totally* closer and *totally* more intense. *(Beat.)* Has Mom seen it? Is she up? She's gotta see it, I've never seen … *(Beat.)* What's going on? (Hi.)

7

MICHAEL. Jeremy, this is Sheriff Egan. *(Short pause.)*

JEREMY. Oh, *shit,* Dad! You *didn't!* You called the fucking cops on me — !

MICHAEL. Jeremy —

JEREMY. *(To Egan.)* We had *a* beer. *One* beer. Not even a beer, we *split* one beer. God, Dad, I can't *believe* you sometimes!

MICHAEL. Jeremy — your mother's missing. *(Short pause.)*

JEREMY. What?

MICHAEL. She's not here, we don't know where she is.

JEREMY. Oh. Well … I mean, maybe she's out, you know … driving. Out looking at the sky. You know she does that. *(To Egan.)* Did he tell you? That she goes up to the mountains sometimes to look at the — the constellations. He may not have told you because he doesn't like it, he doesn't understand it.

MICHAEL. Come on, Jer —

JEREMY. You don't!

EGAN. He told me. We hope that's all it is.

JEREMY. God, if — if something happened to her — *(To Michael.)* This is because of you, you know. For agreeing to — *(To Egan.)* She *never* used to go out at night — when we lived in a city. But this — Fucking *nowhere* in fucking backwater *Virginia!*

MICHAEL. All right, that's —

JEREMY. DID YOU *ONCE* GO WITH HER?! Did you ever *want* to go with her?! Did you ever *ask* her to please not go?

MICHAEL. Jeremy — *(Mini-beat as he realizes it.)* — are you drunk?

JEREMY. Huh? *(Beat.) No.* No, I'm not fucking drunk! Jesus!

MICHAEL. *Fine* — you're upset, then. Go to bed. We'll talk in the morning.

JEREMY. Oh, yeah, I'll definitely just — go to sleep. While Mom's —

MICHAEL. I mean it, Jeremy.

JEREMY. Jesus, you don't even care! You don't even fucking — !

MICHAEL. *That's* — *enough!* (Beat.) I'm not kidding, Jeremy, go to bed. *(A tense beat, then Jeremy starts off, stops, turns back. He is very upset. Maybe crying a little bit.)*

JEREMY. Dad … Dad, I'm sorry —

MICHAEL. It's okay, Jer, it's all right.

JEREMY. I didn't mean —

MICHAEL. I know you didn't, son.

JEREMY. What … what if Mom comes home tonight?

MICHAEL. Then I'll wake you, I will.

JEREMY. Okay, and what if she doesn't?

MICHAEL. Jeremy — *(Beat.)* Then she'll come home tomorrow, all right? Go to sleep. *(Jeremy exits. Michael grimaces.)* He's like this — stranger, living in our house.

EGAN. Mr. Cleary —

MICHAEL. His thing is that he's always threatening to run away, to go back —

EGAN. Mr. Cleary —

MICHAEL. — home, to Washington. Which he has before, several times. He hops a bus or — once, he hitch-hiked, if you can imagine it, and it takes one of us driving and physically dragging him — or he gets bored, and slowly *meanders* his way back —

EGAN. Mr. Cleary —

MICHAEL. I know he was drunk, Sheriff.

EGAN. Your son wasn't drunk.

MICHAEL. He's sixteen, it's not —

EGAN. Did you see his eyes? *(Beat.)* I think your son is taking drugs, Mr. Cleary. *(Beat.)* I think he'd taken drugs earlier this evening. Maybe crystal meth. (We have a problem with that here, with kids taking it when they're bored, for the boredom. It's … an escape here.) *(Michael sits down on the couch again. He puts his head in his hands.)*

MICHAEL. Oh, God …

EGAN. Sometimes kids tell each other things they won't tell us. My son goes to school with your son. I can ask him if he knows anything. And maybe this is a one-time thing, maybe it's not a problem.

MICHAEL. I'd — appreciate that, thank you. *(Beat.)* What's your son's name?

EGAN. Matt, Matthew.

MICHAEL. And he and Jeremy, they're classmates?

EGAN. Yes.

MICHAEL. How come you know that and I don't? *(Egan shrugs.)* How come we've never met?

EGAN. I suspect it's difficult for you. To meet people. Moving here and meeting people.

MICHAEL. Very, yes.

EGAN. That's understandable, even after …

9

MICHAEL. Half a year. Barely. *(Looking around, realizing it.)* Look at us, we're still unpacking …

EGAN. And you decided to move from Washington? Or did your wife — ?

MICHAEL. We both decided. My wife's from here, she grew up in these mountains, she always missed them. I said who needs mountains when you've got all these great — monuments. She hated how it never got dark in the city, not even in the dead of night. There were always lights, she said, from neon signs, the street lamps, making it hard to see the sky. *(Beat.)* I wanted to move because *she* wanted to, and because my job — Because I can do my job anywhere.

EGAN. Deliver milk?

MICHAEL. Well, write, I'm a writer. The milk is more something to, to get out of the house — out of my head — and to give Bridget some time to — *(Beat.)* Because she's also a writer. She's actually working on something. *(Short pause.)* I'm … being remarkably calm about all this, don't you think?

EGAN. If you can, try to get some sleep, Mr. Cleary.

MICHAEL. Should I be doing anything? *Can* I be doing anything?

EGAN. Staying put. I'll come by tomorrow morning. If anything happens tonight, call me. You have the number?

MICHAEL. Yes. *(Feels in his shirt pocket.)* Yes, right here.

EGAN. These back roads are — well, tricky, sometimes. You think you know them, you've driven down them a hundred times, and then they — change on you. Depending on the time of day, on the light. Hopefully your wife's just lost somewhere, waiting till morning, staying put …

MICHAEL. Thank you.

EGAN. Get some sleep, Mr. Cleary. Try. *(Blackout. Lights up on the living room again, the next morning. Michael is pouring milk into a bowl of cereal. It is very early. Jeremy comes in, wearing a T-shirt, boxer shorts.)*

JEREMY. Has Mom — ? Did she — ?

MICHAEL. Not yet. You slept?

JEREMY. Some, yeah. A little, not that much, you know, but some … *(Jeremy sits at the table, pours himself a bowl of cereal. Takes a spoonful. Then:)* I made a list. Of all the places she could be. Of the places she's taken me, the places she's told me about. The ravines, the gorges, the — That the police should probably check.

Or, you know, we can. I wrote them down.

MICHAEL. I wish we'd given that to Egan last night.

JEREMY. Who?

MICHAEL. Egan, the sheriff, you met him last night.

JEREMY. Oh — yeah. *(Eats some cereal.)* I think, maybe, I was pretty … messed up last night. I think, maybe, that I was a little drunk — do you think?

MICHAEL. That was really shitty timing, Jeremy.

JEREMY. I know, Dad.

MICHAEL. We're not gonna have a huge fight about this, we're not gonna *argue* —

JEREMY. I'm sorry, Dad.

MICHAEL. — there's just gonna be a new rule, starting right now. Whatever you did last night, whatever you *took* —

JEREMY. I told you: I had *one* beer.

MICHAEL. — whatever you *took,* Jeremy — I'm not an idiot, all right? — listen to me: If you take it again, if I *catch* you taking it again, if I *think* you've taken it again —

JEREMY. Dad —

MICHAEL. — I believe you know what'll happen, right? *(Beat.)* Jeremy? *(Beat.)* Right?

JEREMY. Yes — right — okay.

MICHAEL. Your mother's missing —

JEREMY. I know.

MICHAEL. And you're off doing —

JEREMY. Dad, I'm sorry! *(Beat.)* Okay? (Jesus …) What do — uhm — the police say? Sheriff — whatever his name is? *(Under his breath.)* Jesus Christ, a fucking sheriff …

MICHAEL. His name's *Benjamin Egan.* And he hasn't said anything, he hasn't come by yet.

JEREMY. Well, did you tell *Benjamin Egan* why Mom goes out at night? Did you tell him what she goes looking for?

MICHAEL. This wasn't at night, this was during the day.

JEREMY. I know, *but did you tell him?*

MICHAEL. *Jeremy* — *(Beat.)* — I don't think telling Egan that your mother's writing a book about space, and black holes, and — and — and —

JEREMY. Aliens.

MICHAEL. — and that *that's* why she goes out at night — I don't think that will help him help us in any way. Do you? *(Beat.)* I think, in fact, that he would probably start making assumptions about her that would —

JEREMY. You're just — you're acting so — how can you be so calm? *(A knock on the front door. Michael and Jeremy freeze. They look. Egan is cracking the door open.)*

EGAN. Mr. Cleary? Can I — ?

MICHAEL. Yes, please. Come in. Is there anything? Have you found — ?

EGAN. Your wife's car — your car — just over an hour ago. On a road off Route 17, down near O'Bannon's mill. Two kids from the high school found it.

JEREMY. *(Perking up.)* Who?

EGAN. *(Ignoring this from Jeremy.)* Its lights were on, its head-lights, and its interior light, too. The door on the driver's side was open, wide open, and resting on the passenger's side, buckled in, was a bag of groceries from the Farmer's Market. Also, your wife's purse was in the car, on the floor, on the passenger's side, and the keys were in the ignition.

MICHAEL. And Bridget?

EGAN. Not yet.

MICHAEL. Jesus …

EGAN. No, Mr. Cleary, listen to me: Finding her car means she didn't wreck it last night. And because her purse was there, it means she wasn't the victim of a robbery. *Not* finding her means she's out there still.

JEREMY. She is — totally.

EGAN. I'm gonna need your help, your son's help, Mr. Cleary. We're pulling together some men —

JEREMY. I have a list, I made a list, of places — locations — where my mom sometimes goes. At night. I have it upstairs.

EGAN. That's great, that's good thinking.

JEREMY. Hang on, let me — I'll — *(Jeremy exits.)*

MICHAEL. She's alive. My wife *is* alive. She's out there lost … but she's alive.

EGAN. We're all working on that assumption —

MICHAEL. NOT an assumption! *(Beat.)* Not — an assumption. She is.

EGAN. Of course. *(Michael nods.)*

MICHAEL. I have to do something now, I can't just — sit here calling people.

EGAN. Come with us — I understand — be part of the search team.

MICHAEL. That's — Thank you.

EGAN. You can help put up posters — hell, you can even make the poster — a Missing Persons poster.

MICHAEL. — all right.

EGAN. I'll put you in touch with the radio stations, the TV stations. You can go on the air, talk about your wife. Show a photograph to cast the widest net possible.

MICHAEL. Yes — great — done. *(Jeremy returns, finishing getting dressed as he comes in. He's got a sheet of paper, which he gives to Egan.)*

JEREMY. Those are what I thought of. I can't — If I think of anything else ...

EGAN. *(Looking over the list.)* No, this is good work, this is very — Thank you, this is great.

JEREMY. So, like, should I go to school? And basketball practice? Or should I come with you?

MICHAEL. Go to school, then come back here. Someone should be here — *(Turns to Egan.)* — is that right?

EGAN. It would be best.

JEREMY. Okay. *(Nods.)* Okay, I'll go and come back. *(Jeremy starts to head for the front door. He's putting on a jacket.)*

EGAN. Hang on, before you — *(Jeremy stops, turns back.)* The lights you saw last night, can you talk about them? Describe them?

JEREMY. Uhm. *(Genuinely baffled.)* What?

EGAN. You said you saw lights in the sky. Last night. You said the sky was — *(He checks his notebook.)* — "all these strange — all these crazy lights and colors."

JEREMY. *I* said that?

EGAN. Something like that. I wrote it down.

JEREMY. Well, I mean ... Uhm. *(Straining to remember.)* Yeah, there *were* weird lights, I guess. *(Beat.)* I don't know, I can't — remember much. I was — tired, you know?

EGAN. Right. Tired.

JEREMY. But if anything comes back to me ...

EGAN. *(Turning to Michael.)* We had a lot of reports last night about lights in the sky. The TV station got some calls, and up at the college, people saying they had seen — *(Beat.)* If your wife saw those lights or heard about them — you said she's a "backyard astronomer" — she might've stayed out to see them.

MICHAEL. What were they?

EGAN. Alien spacecrafts. *(Michael and Jeremy freeze. Egan smiles.)* That's our little joke. Around the station. Whenever we can't explain something. *(Beat, explaining.)* Because we're in Virginia, in the mountains. *(Beat.)* Where one out of every four persons claims to have been abducted. *(Beat. Clears his throat.)* No one knows, we're checking, we're calling people back. We're a small department, bear with us.

JEREMY. I'm gonna be — (Yeah, okay.) — late.

MICHAEL. *(As Jeremy starts to go.)* I'll see you tonight. *(Jeremy exits. Michael looks at Egan.)* We talked this morning, before you came in. He feels terrible.

EGAN. I read some of your book last night.

MICHAEL. You did? My book?

EGAN. Yes.

MICHAEL. Of my book?

EGAN. My wife had it.

MICHAEL. She had my book?

EGAN. We do read in Green Bank, Mr. Cleary, some of us.

MICHAEL. No, that's not — I just never think of anyone ever having read my book. Any — strangers.

EGAN. I'm gonna finish it, if I can. (Though it's not very pleasant, is it?)

MICHAEL. Uhhhh …

EGAN. And I'm gonna order a copy of your wife's book. Unless — you have one I can borrow?

MICHAEL. Upstairs in the attic, boxes of them. I'll get you one.

EGAN. Good. Do that — then we'll go.

MICHAEL. Go…?

EGAN. To meet the search party, Mr. Cleary, and hopefully find your wife. *(Quick blackout. Then there is darkness, the living room in darkness, and lonely night sounds. Crickets, the wind. Jeremy enters from upstairs.)*

JEREMY. Dad? *(Silence.)* Dad, are you — ? *(Movement in the dark, and then the lamp next to the sofa is clicked on. Michael is sitting there.)* It's four in the morning, Dad.

MICHAEL. When someone disappears — (Egan told me this today while we were picking through the fields, the tall grass, down by the mines.) When someone disappears, every hour that passes, the longer they're missing, the less chance they'll come back or be found alive. *(Nods.)* If you don't find them that first hour, those

14

first few hours, your chances drop precipitously. *(Beat.)* *Their* chances drop precipitously.

JEREMY. Should I call someone, Dad? Grandma? Should I call her, do you — ?

MICHAEL. I already did, Jer, when I got back from the search, before they put me on the — the news. *(Shakes his head.)* She's furious I'm not coming to get her, that I'm not sending someone for her.

JEREMY. Maybe we should. I mean, Mom's her daugh —

MICHAEL. *(Interrupting.)* — I can't take care of your grandmother, *and* help Egan find your mother, *and* worry about you, *and* not — come apart, all right? *(Jeremy gets it.)* As soon as we know anything, we'll get her. I'll go — or you will — or someone.

JEREMY. Uhm, Dad? If you're thinking —

MICHAEL. I don't understand — *(Shakes his head, helplessly.)* — I'm not sure why this is happening, Jeremy.

JEREMY. She's on a trip. *(He nods his head quickly.)* Mom is, she won one of those contests, you know? The kind where you pack your bags and you show up at the supermarket for the drawing, and then they pick a name out of a fishbowl, and if they pick your name, you win. But you have to be ready to leave right then, they drive you right to the airport — that's why they ask you to bring your passport — and you get on a plane and you don't stop flying until you're in, like, Australia. They don't even give you time to call your family to tell them you're going. And then when you're there, it's so great, the sun feels so good on your skin, you forget to call, and then you forget you forgot, and the next time you think about your family, you're at the airport, Sydney International Airport or wherever, and you buy these really cheap T-shirts to make up for it. An "I Heart Koala Bears" T-shirt or whatever. *(Short pause.)* She's okay, she's on a trip.

MICHAEL. Jer —

JEREMY. Come upstairs, Dad, you gotta sleep.

MICHAEL. When she comes back, when she opens the door, I want to be the first thing she sees, so she knows we were waiting for her.

JEREMY. Okay. Okay, well, I'm — I'll leave you alone, then, okay? *(Jeremy starts out.)*

MICHAEL. Do you know, Jeremy, I almost didn't marry your mother? You know this story?

JEREMY. Uh … no, Dad. *(Mini-beat.)* This is the most sharing we've done, like, ever. *(Jeremy sits down across from his dad.)*

15

MICHAEL. It wasn't us, we were in love, but her father, your grandfather, said don't do it. To me. When I asked for his permission, when I drove here to Green Bank — well, just outside it. To where their farm used to be. *(Remembers.)* That car ride was … *(Michael gets lost in the memory.)*

JEREMY. Dad?

MICHAEL. Very, very — lonely. It took me all night. I pulled up to your granddad's farm at … oh, God, it was late. At three, maybe four in the morning … this hour … and I just — I sat back and waited. And thought. About your mother. *(Short pause.)* When something makes you happy, Jeremy, the happiest you've ever been, fear … creeps in, underneath the happiness — colors it. "This won't last." "This isn't real." "You don't deserve this."

JEREMY. How long did you wait?

MICHAEL. Until he got up, your granddad. Which was not much time, it was — Oh, before five in the morning. *(Beat.)* When I saw him opening the barn doors, sliding them open, I waved and walked over to him, and he said: "I could use some help with the cows." And he knew what I was up to, he wasn't a stupid man, your grandfather. On the contrary, he was very, very — *(Beat.)* I expected him to, to *object* because of our age, say we were too young, which your mom was, she was barely out of school, and I was ready for that, but before I said anything, *he* said: "I don't think it's a good idea for you to marry Bridget. She's — off, Michael, her eyes are off."

JEREMY. What, what did you do?

MICHAEL. I said, respectfully, "I appreciate that, sir, but I love your daughter, and we *are* getting married." At which point, he nodded, and hugged me. "You're a good man, Michael. For your sake, I hope she grows out of her queerness."

JEREMY. Uhm, what — what did Granddad mean? *(Michael shrugs, thinks for a moment.)*

MICHAEL. There were some things, but … *(Shrugs again.)* Well, she used to sleepwalk, when she was younger. (Wandering the halls like a — ghost.) And not just that, but she didn't — and doesn't still — need much sleep, a few hours each night, four at the most. And she's always cold, always feeling the cold more — acutely. *(Beat.)* You're like that, too.

JEREMY. Sometimes, yeah. *(Short pause.)* Try not to be scared, Dad. I don't think Mom's dead —

MICHAEL. Jeremy —

JEREMY. — or hurt. I think — or maybe I just feel it — but I think something really great, really unbelievably *amazing* is happening to her. *(The lights dim, shift, come on strong. It's the next day. Sun is streaming in through the window. Egan is sitting in the living room alone. The phone on the desk starts ringing ... and ringing. Egan just stares at it. The front door opens, Michael comes in, rushes to the phone, answers.)*

MICHAEL. Hello? Hello? Hello? *(There's no response, so Michael hangs up, immediately starts unbuttoning his shirt.)*

EGAN. The door was open —

MICHAEL. *(Shocked, scared.)* JESUS CHRIST!

EGAN. I let myself in. I hope —

MICHAEL. Sheriff — Jesus — !

EGAN. Who was on the phone?

MICHAEL. Oh — uh — nobody. It's been — doing that. Ringing — and then I answer — and then ... nothing. No static, just a silence, a dead —

EGAN. Someone's seen your wife — *saw* her — the day she went missing. *(Explaining.)* That's where I've been. That's why I wasn't with you, with the search party.

MICHAEL. What? Who did?

EGAN. A woman, a waitress at a bar called Dietle's Place.

MICHAEL. Saw Bridget?

EGAN. Says she did. *Thinks* she did, at least. This woman — her name's Angela Stone — recognized her from the picture you showed on the broadcast and called me.

MICHAEL. What — (She did?) — what did she say?

EGAN. Lots of things, she's a talker, but to begin with that your wife went there ... many times.

MICHAEL. To this bar called Dieder's — ?

EGAN. Dietle's Place. Yes.

MICHAEL. Which I've never heard of.

EGAN. Well, it's not really a place for locals, for ... your kind of folks. The men who go there — truckers and day workers, you know — they go there for drinks, to cool off with drinks, and sometimes ... *(Beat.)* Your son's at school still? *(Michael nods his head, then asks:)*

MICHAEL. At basketball practice. Does she know where Bridget is, this woman? Did you ask her?

EGAN. She says your wife — (this is hard, Mr. Cleary) — but she says that your wife … went with the men there. Went … off with them.

MICHAEL. I'm sorry, Sheriff, but I — ahm — I don't understand what you — what she — *(Beat.)* Why would Bridget — *where* would Bridget "go off" with them?

EGAN. The parking lot — *(Mini-beat.)* — she says. (I'm sorry.) And their trucks, sometimes. And sometimes to motels, further down Route 80. *(Beat.)* The last time Angela Stone saw your wife — she thinks, she can't be sure — was not even a week ago, right before she disappeared, when she … went off with two men.

MICHAEL. No. Not my — My wife wouldn't —

EGAN. Of course she wouldn't. *(Beat.)* Even so, Mr. Cleary, we should probably —

MICHAEL. This woman — this Angela person — how well do you know her, Sheriff?

EGAN. I just met her.

MICHAEL. So she could be mistaken. Or — or lying. It's conceivable, I mean, that for some reason she wants to — she's trying to — hurt Bridget.

EGAN. Why would she be trying to hurt your wife?

MICHAEL. Or damage her reputation! Or —

EGAN. Whatever her intentions, I'm gonna need you to talk to this woman.

MICHAEL. WHY? I fucking — *(Mini-beat.)* — I *know* my wife, Sheriff. My wife is — she's missing, could be hurt somewhere, could be worse than hurt — and this waitress is, what? Making up stories? Damaging — ? *(Beat.)* You know these people. There's nothing happening in their own lives, they're so desperate for — for — *anything,* they'll do *anything* to pump themselves up. You should see — they stop me on the street — these people who hadn't ever looked at me twice. Asking for — offering — Because they want to touch this. Be a part of, of the story.

EGAN. Not this woman, she's decent. You'd see that. Which — that's why I think you should sit down with her.

MICHAEL. What are you saying about my wife, Sheriff? About me? *(Silence in the living room.)* Even if this woman were telling the truth, would that change anything? Would we stop looking for Bridget?

EGAN. — no.

MICHAEL. Bridget did *not* go off with anyone. That is not my

18

wife — not a thing my wife would do. I'd believe anything else before I'd believe that, Sheriff.

EGAN. I understand that, but this is still our first — *(Unsaid: "— lead.")*

MICHAEL. I AM TELLING YOU: Whomever that woman saw — it was someone else, someone who may *look* like my wife —

EGAN. All right.

MICHAEL. — but it isn't Bridget. Wasn't. Believe me. *(Pause, as Egan regards Michael with a mixture of sympathy and pity.)*

EGAN. We'll go out tomorrow — again, in the morning — and we'll spend the day looking. But Mr. Cleary … Tomorrow, or the day after at the latest, you're gonna have to meet with this waitress and hear what she has to say. *(After a few moments, Michael nods his head, and the lights fade. When they come back up, it is the next day, almost dusk. Jeremy's there, holding a stack of large, old-fashioned scrapbooks, stuffed to bursting with clippings. He's waiting for his dad to come home. Which, after a few moments, he does — Michael enters — angry.)*

JEREMY. Dad —

MICHAEL. Nothing! Six hours, pushing through the woods —

JEREMY. Dad —

MICHAEL. Six hours with the search party, going over the same goddamn fields —

JEREMY. Dad —

MICHAEL. The same —

JEREMY. *Dad* —

MICHAEL. *What,* Jeremy?

JEREMY. Uhm. *(Deep breath.)* I was just gonna do my comic books — you know, organize them, put them in alphabetical order, separate the Marvels from the DCs — and then get all my sports stuff in one place. So that when Mom comes back, I could show her that I'd cleaned my share of the attic, at least. And … I wasn't planning on opening any of her boxes, or going through her trunk, which I know is, like, a *total* invasion of privacy, and you can get mad at me if you want, but I did, and, uh —

MICHAEL. You went through your mother's trunk?

JEREMY. Yeah, and — brace yourself, Dad, but — *(Beat.)* — I think Mom believes in aliens. *(Short pause.)*

MICHAEL. She's writing a book about them, she doesn't believe in them.

JEREMY. No, Dad. She actually — *seriously* — does.

MICHAEL. *(Sighing.)* Jeremy —

JEREMY. She's been collecting some weird — And making these bizarre notes, these surreal — drawings. *(He holds up the scrapbook.)* This is the most recent one, the most recent — scrapbook. They're all dated. Like journals, journal entries. *(Jeremy gives the book to his dad.)* They go back years, like she's been doing this for years.

MICHAEL. *(Flipping through the book.)* It's research to *refute* their existence, not —

JEREMY. No, Dad, the articles? They're from different papers, from all over the country. About crop circles — about people "missing time" — people going to sleep in one place and waking up somewhere else, in a different city, in a different country — articles about Roswell, New Mexico, the crash site — pictures of autopsies — stories about secret government agencies, government cover-ups, global conspiracies —

MICHAEL. This doesn't mean anything, Jeremy, it doesn't prove —

JEREMY. No, Dad, all of her nocturnal — whatevers? Not for inspiration, not to look at stars — *to make contact.*

MICHAEL. Jeremy, I've spent the last six hours —

JEREMY. But that's what I'm *saying,* Dad: If they exist, and if Mom hooked up with them or whatever, you're not gonna find her in some — some ditch. Some field. I'm telling you: people — *(Mini-beat.)* — they believe. *(Beat.)* I don't *not* believe. What Mom wrote — *(Jeremy takes the scrapbook back from his father.)* "As there are about one billion stars in our galaxy, the number of planets would be about ten billion. After elimination of frozen planets and planets sterilized by heat, there are approximately ten million likely planets in the galaxy suitable for life."

MICHAEL. Jer —

JEREMY. "We must explore *all* possibilities *always,* beginning with the possibility that intelligent life is abundant and, in fact, occurs on every planet." *(Closes the book.)* She's, like, *fanatical.*

MICHAEL. Don't say that. Your mother's not —

JEREMY. She wrote down conversations she's had with the aliens, Dad, entire conversations. Dialogue. Pages and pages of stuff. *Years* of work. *(Michael takes one of the scrapbooks, starts looking through it.)*

MICHAEL. No, Jeremy, this is — these are — they're transcriptions of interviews, interviews she's conducted with —

JEREMY. Aliens.

MICHAEL. — *No,* with people who claim to have been abducted, who believe they've had contact with —

JEREMY. Aliens.

MICHAEL. — with *something,* but *we* don't know what, and *they* don't know what.

JEREMY. Okay, Dad, you remember last night? I told you I felt something amazing was happening to Mom?

MICHAEL. Yes.

JEREMY. Okay, so what if this is it? What if they're real, and they — they took her?

MICHAEL. Who?

JEREMY. The aliens.

MICHAEL. Stop it. There are no — *(A knock on the front door. Uh-oh. Michael and Jeremy freeze.)*

JEREMY. IT'S THEM, IT'S THE ALIENS!

MICHAEL. Jeremy — *(Another knock.)* Get this — get all this nonsense out of here.

EGAN. *(From the other side of the front door.)* CLEARY, IT'S EGAN.

JEREMY. They're like chameleons, like — shape-shifters, she wrote. He could be one of them. Egan. Always showing up here? Creeping around? According to what Mom wrote, some of them can —

MICHAEL. JEREMY! *(Picks up a load of journals, stuffs them into his son's arms.)* Take these books and get upstairs.

JEREMY. But we have to tell —

MICHAEL. If we tell Egan that your mother talks to aliens — that she even *thinks* she talks to aliens — he will stop taking this seriously, he will stop looking for her, she will be one more poster to him, that's all — Do you understand? Do you want that?

JEREMY. I'm just — *(Mini-beat.)* No.

EGAN. *(Offstage.)* Cleary, will you open — ?

MICHAEL. Hang on — ! Give me one — ! *(To Jeremy.)* Get these upstairs. Don't say anything. Don't tell anyone —

JEREMY. — all right.

MICHAEL. Go.

JEREMY. All right! *(Jeremy exits upstairs, carrying all the scrapbooks. Still rattled a bit, Michael opens the front door, letting Egan into the living room.)*

MICHAEL. Sorry about that, my son —

EGAN. Where is he?

MICHAEL. Upstairs. Why, did you find — ?

EGAN. Tell me you're decent — tell me I'm not wrong about you.

MICHAEL. Sheriff...?

EGAN. If you had any information, anything that might help us find your wife — you'd tell me, wouldn't you? You want us to find her, don't you?

MICHAEL. Of course. Sheriff —

EGAN. There's nothing you'd keep from me? For any reason? To protect anyone — protect yourself?

MICHAEL. Of course not, of course I'd tell you. *(Egan takes this in, nods his head once, then speaks.)*

EGAN. This college kid, at the station. Who does our paperwork. Dan McFarland — he helped with your poster.

MICHAEL. I remember, yes.

EGAN. He has a brother, who's a policeman.

MICHAEL. Yes?

EGAN. In Washington, D.C. *(Pause as Michael takes this in.)* Dan faxed his brother a request: "Do you have anything on Michael or Bridget Cleary? They lived in D.C. until about six months ago." The most basic policing. Which I failed to do. *(Beat.)* I can read you the police report they faxed back to him.

MICHAEL. No. You don't have —

EGAN. Are you sure? 'Cause I don't want there to be any more *confusion* between us, I don't want there to be any more *secrets. (Beat.)* It's about you and your wife, of course. *(Beat.)* It describes a domestic dispute between you and your wife. *(Beat.)* Who was treated for injuries that included a broken nose and a concussion.

MICHAEL. *(Quiet.)* ... yes.

EGAN. I had the tiniest suspicion in my head, when you first called me. *(Beat.)* But then when I met you, when I saw you, I thought there was no way you could've done anything to your wife. Not the way you were talking about her, the way you looked.

MICHAEL. It only happened — once, Sheriff.

EGAN. Do you know how many husbands only hit their wives once? *(A challenge; Michael has nothing to say.)* If that's true, why not tell me, then, why hide it?

MICHAEL. I wasn't —

EGAN. *Did you honestly think it wasn't important?*

MICHAEL. Lower your voice, Jeremy's upstairs, and he —

EGAN. Doesn't know?

MICHAEL. No — Sheriff — could you? — sit down. *(Egan doesn't.)*

22

Please. *(He still doesn't.) Please,* Sheriff. *(Egan does.)* Go ahead and investigate me, I haven't done anything to Bridget. I want her back safe more than anything else I've ever —

EGAN. Then stop *lying* to me!

MICHAEL. I didn't, I'm not —

EGAN. Why won't you meet with Angela Stone?

MICHAEL. Who?

EGAN. The waitress from Dietle's Place — why won't you hear her story?

MICHAEL. I —

EGAN. Do you think it's true? That your wife goes behind your back — went behind your back?

MICHAEL. No —

EGAN. Has she before? Is that why you — ?

MICHAEL. Sheriff, *please* —

EGAN. If there's anything you're withholding, Cleary — anything *else* — before it's too late —

MICHAEL. It was the most cowardly thing I've ever done. Which I wake up with every morning, Sheriff, and carry with me every — *(Beat.)* Which happened because I thought — I *did* think — that Bridget was ... But she wasn't doing anything. (It was a horrendous ...) But Bridget forgave me.

EGAN. For striking her?

MICHAEL. I didn't tell you because everyone — every couple (you know this, Sheriff) — has something between them, some secret, that ties them together. This — what I did to Bridget — was ours, the invisible piece of rope we carried between us. Until ... *(Michael shakes his head.)* I can't feel it anymore.

EGAN. What, Mr. Cleary?

MICHAEL. The rope. Like Bridget's let it drop from her hand. And why would she do that unless she were ... *(Beat.)* Today, while we were out searching, as we were walking along the river, dragging those — those poles through the water, trying to — to snag something, anything — it welled up in me: the feeling that it was over. *(Jeremy's there, he's just walked in.)*

JEREMY. You think Mom's dead?

MICHAEL. Jeremy —

JEREMY. Mom's not dead, Dad, she's — *(Jeremy points. Michael and Egan turn to look at the front door. Bridget Cleary is there. She is a beautiful woman. She is closing the door behind her.)*

BRIDGET. I'm so … I had to go with them … For us, for our family … *(Michael goes to his wife, hugs her. Jeremy is standing apart from his mom and dad.)*

JEREMY. I, like, *told* you, Dad … *(Egan looks from the couple, to Jeremy, as — the lights slowly fade. When they come back up, Egan is gone. It is later that night; dark outside. Bridget is sitting on the couch. Nearby, also sitting down, are Michael and Jeremy. After a long, establishing pause:)*

BRIDGET. I had no way of, of communicating with you. Or else I would've called you, I would've done *something*. I had my phone. I tried to use it, but it didn't work where I was, and they … don't have …

MICHAEL. Who? Who were you with? Who were these people?

BRIDGET. Not people, Michael, they're … *(A short pause, then:)*

MICHAEL. Bridget — honey?

BRIDGET. They're not human, they're … *(But, as usual, Jeremy has to utter the unutterable:)*

JEREMY. Aliens — and they don't have phones 'cause they don't *use* phones, they use…?

BRIDGET. Telepathy.

MICHAEL. Excuse me?

BRIDGET. To communicate. With each other. With us, they use a kind of … crude sign language — or drawings sometimes.

JEREMY. Like Pictionary?

BRIDGET. Something like that. Our brains aren't advanced enough — the way we order our thoughts is so underdeveloped — they can't read our minds they way they read each other's. *(Michael turns to Jeremy.)*

MICHAEL. *Now* do you see why I didn't tell Egan? Why I made him leave? If he heard *any* of this —

BRIDGET. He could've stayed, he could've heard this —

MICHAEL. Well, sure, because there's *nothing* strange about you having been abducted, out of the blue, by —

BRIDGET. No, not abducted, *asked*. And not out of the blue, either, there was nothing sudden about it. *(Beat.)* All my life, I've known — I've suspected — that something like this would happen to me eventually.

MICHAEL. Really? All your life?

BRIDGET. Since I was a girl, yes. Sensing that there was something more, something — *beyond*. What we knew. Us, humanity, the stars.

Something *else*. A feeling that I was alone … and *not* alone.

JEREMY. How old were you, Mom?

BRIDGET. When they first started appearing to me?

JEREMY. Yeah — yes.

BRIDGET. It was only in my dreams, at first …

MICHAEL. Stop it, Bridget, please stop this. You don't believe in them, you've *never* believed in —

BRIDGET. I never told you, I never told anyone, but … I did. I *do* believe. I *have* to. *(Beat, turns to her son.)* I was younger than you, Jeremy, the first time. I thought they were fairies … or angels … or … I had no idea *what* they were until I got older, and they began to … They talk without using their mouths. Some of them don't even have mouths. They live … *(Shakes her head.)* … we can't *measure* how long they live. Their eyes register light that's invisible to us, light that exists beyond either end of the spectrum. Their bodies weigh so little, like birds, their bones are hollow. They … fly almost. Like … stars.

JEREMY. What color are they? In your scrapbooks — *(Beat. Uh-oh.)*

BRIDGET. My what?

JEREMY. Nothing.

BRIDGET. You went through my scrapbooks? In my trunk? Jeremy?

JEREMY. Uhm. I mean, accidentally I did, yeah.

BRIDGET. Michael?

MICHAEL. Yes, and — for the record — that's not the only *infraction* your little boy committed while you were away —

JEREMY. Dad —

BRIDGET. What?

MICHAEL. Ask your son.

JEREMY. Okay, Dad, you — *suck.*

BRIDGET. What is he talking about? Jeremy?

JEREMY. Okay — (Jesus …) — okay, *fine.* The night you were, like, abducted —

BRIDGET. I wasn't abducted, why does everyone keep saying — ?

JEREMY. Okay, fine — the night you *willingly went away with the aliens and didn't call because they don't have phones,* I was out with friends, and we had — *I* had — one beer. To drink. Okay?

BRIDGET. Michael?

MICHAEL. A beer — or possibly something stronger and more illegal.

25

BRIDGET. Oh, Jeremy —

JEREMY. Okay, Mom? Before you say anything — or, like, cry — Dad already chewed me out, okay? *(Beat.)* And, like, why am *I* suddenly the one on trial?

MICHAEL. You're sixteen, you're *always* on trial.

JEREMY. We were talking about *aliens* — about what color they are? Because in your books, in the artists' renditions or whatever, sometimes they're green, sometimes they're blue, and sometimes they're gray.

BRIDGET. They are like us, they're different colors.

MICHAEL. Oh — well — actually, I don't know anyone who's green, or gray, or blue.

JEREMY. Are they good? Or, like — evil? Like, bad?

MICHAEL. Well, this is just an educated guess, Jeremy, but if they're like us, some must be good and some must be evil. *(To Bridget.)* The ones that took you — kidnapped you — *abducted* you — were they good or bad? Or indifferent?

BRIDGET. They didn't force me, I didn't do anything I didn't want to, it was just … time for me to go with them. They wanted to show me —

MICHAEL. You left your car like you'd been — *(Exasperated.)* You just *left* it, Bridget.

BRIDGET. I wasn't scared at all, they're the most — *(Beat.)* They were standing in the middle of the road. Six of them. It was the first time I'd seen them out during the day. They waved for me to pull over, which I did —

JEREMY. You went with them?

BRIDGET. They took me through a portal — Passing through it felt like … rain on my bare skin.

JEREMY. Where'd you go?

MICHAEL. While we were sitting here, thinking the worst? Imagining — imagining that you — *(Beat.) We thought you were dead!*

JEREMY. Not me.

MICHAEL. *I* thought you were dead, then, *I* did.

JEREMY. Okay, Dad? Chill.

MICHAEL. Where, Bridget? And don't — lie.

BRIDGET. A place like the Earth … and *not* like the Earth. Completely unspoiled. Where they're gonna start again, their great experiment. *(Beat.)* They wanted me to see where Jeremy would be living.

JEREMY. Me?

BRIDGET. You're one of the people they've chosen — hand-picked — for their project.

JEREMY. Me?

MICHAEL. For what?

BRIDGET. They need one hundred people to — to populate the new planet.

JEREMY. One hundred of — me?

BRIDGET. No. *(She laughs.)* No, it's a … cross-section of people. Everyone would be different. Men, women — mostly women.

JEREMY. Cool.

MICHAEL. You keep talking about this as if it's real.

BRIDGET. It is.

MICHAEL. Bridget, you — *(He looks at her. Closely. Realizes.)* You believe this.

BRIDGET. I was *there,* Michael. They wanted to get me on their side, so I would hand Jeremy over to them —

MICHAEL. *WHAT ARE YOU TALKING ABOUT? (Short pause.)* You — you don't believe they exist. You've told me, over and over again, *insisted* — you don't believe in them.

BRIDGET. I do. I have. All these years.

MICHAEL. The book, the book you've been working on — You said that refuting their existence was your "way in," do you remember? That it was all about why we *shouldn't* believe in them.

BRIDGET. That was — I was — That wasn't true, Michael, I'm sorry. The book is — There is no — *(Unsaid: " — book.")* You saw what I was doing, what I was collecting, and I said it was for a book, but … there isn't any. Book? No. I lied because they warned me to not tell anyone, not even you, until it was time.

JEREMY. The aliens did?

BRIDGET. *(To Michael.)* In a week, they're coming to get Jeremy. Where there's a clearing in the cornfield at the edge of town — the one Jeremy passes on his way to school — that's where they want him to wait for them. It's all been carefully planned — plotted. Who the hundred people are, when they have to go. They want to create an entirely new human race. *(Beat.)* With Jeremy.

JEREMY. But I've never — I mean — Okay, I'm just gonna — I'm a virgin, okay? *(Beat.)* I mean, I've *kissed* —

MICHAEL. Stop it, Jeremy, you're not going anywhere.

BRIDGET. They thought — because I *believed* in them, because

I was *open* to them —

MICHAEL. But you weren't — you're not —

BRIDGET. — *because I was open to them,* they thought that I would let Jeremy be one of the hundred. That I would *want* it, even. That's why they let me come back here, to help him get ready, but ... *(Turns to her son.)* ... you're not going, Jeremy.

JEREMY. I mean, I should at least consider it, right?

MICHAEL. I want to see one. If they can appear to you, they can appear to me. Call one. Call a — a green one.

BRIDGET. No, Michael.

MICHAEL. Because you can't?

BRIDGET. Because it doesn't matter whether or not you believe. *(Beat.)* God, they were right about you ... *(Beat.)* You don't have to believe. They don't stop being real — what's happening doesn't stop being real — because you don't believe. In not even a week, they will come for Jeremy.

MICHAEL. Our son. Our sixteen-year-old —

JEREMY. Hang on a sec.

BRIDGET. What, honey?

JEREMY. What do we tell the aliens about me not going?

MICHAEL. They're not real, Jeremy, there are — no —

JEREMY. Yeah, but if they *are* real, if they *are* out there, and they *are* coming for me, and I'm *not* going with them ... what happens? I mean, they won't just take me, will they? *(Beat.)* Mom? *(Beat.)* They won't just —

BRIDGET. I don't know. *(Short pause.)* I don't know what they'll do. *(Pause.)*

MICHAEL. Jeremy, would you — ? Could you go to your room, please?

JEREMY. What? Why? I didn't *do* anything this time —

MICHAEL. This isn't a punishment, this is — Your mom and I —

JEREMY. — *fine.* (Jesus.) *(Jeremy starts out.)*

MICHAEL. And don't worry, son — about anything. All right? *(Jeremy nods and exits. After he's gone:)* Are you *trying* to scare him?

BRIDGET. He should, he *should* be afraid. *(Beat, explaining.)* They *would* take him, unless we — *(She decides something.)* — no, we can't stay here. We have to go away with Jeremy and — and hide him. We can go back to Washington, they don't like cities, they're not dark enough, and we'll wait this out, we'll —

MICHAEL. They told you I didn't believe?

BRIDGET. — yes.

MICHAEL. — what *else* did they tell you about me?

BRIDGET. I …

MICHAEL. Bridget.

BRIDGET. They also warned me — said … I should be careful of you. That you might try to … hurt me again.

MICHAEL. *(Quietly.)* … what?

BRIDGET. But you wouldn't, would you?

MICHAEL. No. *(Shakes his head.)* No, never.

BRIDGET. I know you wouldn't. You promised me. That's what I told them, that you prom — *(Bridget stops, sees that Michael isn't moving, that he's fixed his eyes on her and is just staring, staring, staring.)* Michael? What are you doing, what are you thinking?

MICHAEL. I'm … looking at you. *(Beat.)* I'm just — I'm looking at you. *(Lights slowly fade on this image: Michael staring at his wife, not knowing what he's really seeing.)*

End of Act One

ACT TWO

Darkness. Then: A spot of light comes up on Jeremy, who talks to the audience. As he does, the lights slowly rise on the living room. It's afternoon; sun pours in the picture window. Bridget sits by it, her eyes closed, her face turned up to absorb the warmth.

JEREMY. *(To audience.)* Do you ever go out at night to look at the stars? *(Waits for an answer, then:)* It has to be a clear night, and you can't be in the city, you have to be in the country, but with your naked eyes ... you can see more than a thousand stars, floating up there in the black sky ... *(Amending quickly.)* But not at first. At first, you have to let your eyes adjust. It's called "dark adaptation," what happens to your eyes. (My mom told me one time.) Your pupils widen to, like, a quarter of an inch to suck in as much light as possible. And this fluid called "visual purple" — really, "visual purple" — floods your retinas, making them super-sensitive. And you can see in the dark, and ... *(Beat.)* And invisible things come into focus. *(To Bridget.)* Mom — *(Suddenly, Bridget starts, noticing Jeremy for the first time.)*
BRIDGET. Jeremy — oh, God — you — !
JEREMY. Oh, sorry, did I — ?
BRIDGET. How long have you been standing there?
JEREMY. A little while. Sorry, Mom.
BRIDGET. I was resting my eyes, thinking ...
JEREMY. About Dad? *(This surprises Bridget.)*
BRIDGET. You can tell?
JEREMY. I'm disaffected, Mom, not dumb. *(He tries a smile.)* And he is, like, totally freaked.
BRIDGET. He hasn't being sleeping. *(Beat.)* Well, until now; he's upstairs now, tangled in the sheets.
JEREMY. I haven't been sleeping much, either. And then, when I do, I have these ... Like, really disjointed dreams ... Like, I'll be on the beach — (and I'm just a little kid, building a sandcastle or

30

whatever) — and then I'll look up and … *see* one, you know? Looming over me, like a, a jellyfish-person …

BRIDGET. *(Nodding, to herself.)* (Not dreams, memories …)

JEREMY. What?

BRIDGET. Those aren't dreams you're having, they're — *(Beat.)* They saved your life once, Jeremy. You almost died, but they … You were in the first grade, this was at night but not too late, I was in the basement doing laundry, you were upstairs watching cartoons and eating hot dogs —

JEREMY. I never eat hot dogs, Mom —

BRIDGET. You used to. *(Beat.)* You started to choke, and I didn't — *hear* you, but I *felt* something was happening to you. When I ran upstairs, you were blue, and I just — I was rooted. *(Short pause.)* "He's suffocating," I thought, "He's going to die."

JEREMY. You just — froze?

BRIDGET. By the time I started to come out of it, they were already drifting into the room through a window. (They moved like dancers, strange ballet dancers …) They surrounded you on the floor. Four of them. And your eyelids were fluttering, all I could see were their whites, you'd gone from panting, gasping for breath, to … making almost a clicking noise. But one pried opened your mouth — and another made his fingers elongate into tongs — and reached into your mouth, your throat, your windpipe, and pulled out what was choking you.

JEREMY. A — hot dog?

BRIDGET. A third of one, all chewed up.

JEREMY. Jesus, that's — disgusting, I'm sorry you had to see that.

BRIDGET. You were breathing again, your little chest was going up and down, and I just — I started to weep. And one of them, a female one, brushed your hair across your forehead, and her gesture was so … She looked human, completely human. *(Short pause.)* And then they were gone the same way they'd come, out the window.

JEREMY. (Whoa, I just got a chill —)

BRIDGET. You've always had a team protecting you.

JEREMY. Like … bodyguards? *Alien* bodyguards?

BRIDGET. Watching over you your entire life.

JEREMY. Wow, that's so — *(Beat.)* Wait: even in the, like, shower?

BRIDGET. Everywhere.

JEREMY. And you never said anything to me? Or Dad? Or anyone?

BRIDGET. Nothing. *(Short pause.)* Your father and I discovered, early on, that it's better when people only tell each other the things they can accept. That it's easier.

JEREMY. I don't want to go with them.

BRIDGET. You're not, you won't.

JEREMY. You say that, but —

BRIDGET. No, we're not going to be anywhere near this place when they come. I've already let your grandmother know we're staying with her.

JEREMY. Okay, but couldn't we go now? Just to be, you know, on the safe side?

BRIDGET. *(Shaking her head.)* I don't want them to have a chance to — to respond, to come after us. I want them to think everything's fine — that we're following their plan — but — And then we'll slip away, the day before the night they're due to arrive.

JEREMY. The three of us?

BRIDGET. Your father also, yes.

JEREMY. What if he won't let us? Or he doesn't — he won't leave with us?

BRIDGET. I think … we keep trying to convince him, but if he won't … *(She doesn't say what they're both thinking.)*

JEREMY. … right — okay — yeah. *(Bridget and Jeremy are looking at each other, as the lights on them fade. When they come up again, it is night in the living room. Michael is there, a bundle of nervous energy, talking to Egan.)*

MICHAEL. They're at the movies. At the drive-in. Isn't that — ? *(He stops, pauses, starts again.)* It's like we're playing a game: Whoever acts the most normal, the most natural, wins. *(Beat.)* When really it took *everything* in me to let them go. To not scream. To let Jeremy go off with — *whoever* that person is —

EGAN. Your wife.

MICHAEL. No, I'm telling you —

EGAN. I saw her come in, Mr. Cleary. That wasn't an imposter, that wasn't some — *(Looking at Michael closely.)* Mr. Cleary —

MICHAEL. *(Shaking his head.)* You don't understand, you're not understanding me, I'm just starting to understand it my —

EGAN. What?

MICHAEL. At first, my first thought was: "Bridget's gone crazy, she's had a breakdown, or she's been traumatized by something, or she's — " But then — then I started listening to her, and looking at

32

her — *really* looking at her — and I thought about what she was telling me. That she's believed in them her whole life. That she's been lying to me all these years because they told her to. And Bridget — the *real* Bridget — doesn't lie. Wouldn't lie. To me. And — and — *(Mini-beat.)* — do *you* believe in aliens, Sheriff? That they exist?

EGAN. Mr. Cleary …

MICHAEL. You didn't hear her story —

EGAN. You sent me away —

MICHAEL. A mistake — I shouldn't have — I know that now — but some of them can do that, can change their bodies, their forms. Some of them are — are shape-shifters.

EGAN. Some *aliens* are?

MICHAEL. Bridget told me. Or Jeremy did. *(Searching.)* Someone … *(Back on track.)* And about how they're gonna come, come and take him.

EGAN. Who?

MICHAEL. Jeremy. *(Beat.)* Unless we move. (Can you believe that?) She's saying we have to move, go back to D.C., before they come to take Jeremy.

EGAN. Okay, first: No one's taking anyone.

MICHAEL. As she was talking, my wife, as she was telling us this story, I saw her — She was changing. What I knew my wife to be — and what was sitting there, on the couch, talking to us — didn't match, didn't — fit. Was wrong. *(Beat.)* She *isn't* the same person.

EGAN. People change sometimes —

MICHAEL. No, I'm not talking about *changing,* I'm talking about *becoming something else. Being* something else.

EGAN. Which isn't possible. *(Beat.)* It isn't, Mr. Cleary.

MICHAEL. It took me — it's taken me — days. The last five days, the last four nights — I haven't slept. I've stayed awake —

EGAN. *Why?*

MICHAEL. To study her. To *look* at her. Because that's when she — when *it* — most comes into focus. *(Beat.)* Or when it loses focus. *(Beat.)* I think when she's asleep, when she's resting, that's when her defenses are down, and whatever she's projecting to make us *think* she's Bridget stops. *(Going to his desk, to a stack of books there.)* In the books, the books I've been reading, some of them, they practice a kind of … weak mind-control. *(Egan is looking at Michael.)* Don't do that, don't look at me like that, I'm not — crazy.

EGAN. No, but you haven't slept in — how long, four days? On top of what you'd already *not* slept the week before? And the stress, and the fear, and the —

MICHAEL. That's not why I'm — *(Beat.)* Could you sleep in the same bed with a stranger?

EGAN. You're exhausted, Mr. Cleary. Look at yourself, you're shaking. You're not thinking —

MICHAEL. *I am perfectly lucid, Sheriff Egan. (Beat.)* And even someone who hasn't slept in four days knows his wife when he sees her! And I am telling you — again — the person you saw walk through that door is not my wife.

EGAN. People, they sometimes — they even look different.

MICHAEL. Sheriff Egan, please — *(Deep breath.)* — try to think, try to imagine: a person you know, a person you love, someone you've built an entire life with. Imagine waking up one morning and realizing that that person — she's *gone*. And someone else is there, in her place. *(A pause, then Michael continues very slowly, as though he were talking to a small child.)* If my wife wasn't taken, taken and … *(Unsaid: " … replaced?")* Where was she? Those days she was missing?

EGAN. I don't know. Maybe — do you think? — maybe it's time you talked to Angela Stone down at Dietle's Place?

MICHAEL. Why? For what? To hear how — to hear her *malign* — ?

EGAN. — no, to take a step back, Mr. Cleary, and come at this a different way. *(Trying to be reasonable.)* If your wife isn't the person you thought she was, maybe, possibly, she's *this* person. Maybe she's the person who goes out at night, to Dietle's place or wherever, and is living a secret — And — and maybe that's who she's showing you now. And that's why she seems — appears —

MICHAEL. Please, Sheriff, you have to — please listen to me — you have to help me find out what happened to —

EGAN. — *but that's what I'm trying to do! (Beat, thinking this through:)* Look, all right: If your wife really *isn't* your wife —

MICHAEL. She's not, she isn't — !

EGAN. — all right, but if she isn't, and she really is an alien —

MICHAEL. Or something — !

EGAN. — and she says that other aliens are coming to take your son away —

MICHAEL. In three days — *(Correcting himself.)* — not even, in two days!

EGAN. Why would she be trying to protect him, then — hide

him? *(Pause.)* You see, Mr. Cleary? You're not making sense. None of this makes any — Wouldn't she try to keep Jeremy here? Wouldn't she want him to go — to go off with them? *(Short pause as Egan contemplates Michael.)* You know what I think? I think you believe that something happened to your wife —

MICHAEL. *Is* happening. Something terrible —

EGAN. Okay — something terrible. *(Beat, then continuing quickly.)* Which is keeping you awake at night, and disorienting you, and disturbing you, and making you make connections and *see* things that aren't really there, that aren't really happening. Or if they are —

MICHAEL. I *knew* that if I asked for help, no one would — *(Beat.)* Sheriff Egan, something is happening here, to my family, that I can't — that I don't completely understand, but I am asking you to please help me. To believe in me enough to — to keep looking for Bridget, the real Bridget.

EGAN. But I saw —

MICHAEL. All right, *fine:* to help me keep my son safe, then. To look after him, after us — to look at what's happening here — and to help us if we need it. Can you…? Will you?

EGAN. … all right. *(Helpless to say anything else, he repeats:)* … all right, I will. *(Blackout. The lights come up. Morning, the next day. Bridget, wearing an apron, is walking in from the kitchen, setting down a plate of eggs for breakfast. Michael comes down the stairs slowly, sluggishly.)*

MICHAEL. *(Confused, groggy.)* Hello…?

BRIDGET. Morning. Did you sleep?

MICHAEL. Where's — ? Is Jeremy — ?

BRIDGET. At school. *(Beat.)* I'm just making eggs, do you want some?

MICHAEL. I'm not hungry.

BRIDGET. You don't want eggs, I can make you something else.

MICHAEL. My favorite?

BRIDGET. If you'd like. *(She stands, starts to go.)*

MICHAEL. I would, yes — waffles — thank you. *(Bridget stops. Looks at Michael.)* What?

BRIDGET. You *hate* waffles, Michael.

MICHAEL. No, I don't.

BRIDGET. Of course you do, what are you talking about? You *hate* waffles, you *tolerate* pancakes, you *love* French toast with whipped cream and powdered sugar. *They're* your favorite.

35

MICHAEL. Used to be. Were. People change.

BRIDGET. In a week?

MICHAEL. Overnight, sometimes. *(Bridget looks at Michael some more. Then suddenly:)* Have you ever been to a bar called Dietle's Place on Route 80? (Please don't lie.)

BRIDGET. I wouldn't. *(Beat.)* How did you — ?

MICHAEL. Egan told me, Egan found out. A woman who works at — at — at —

BRIDGET. Dietle's bar.

MICHAEL. — says she saw you there — she's seen you there — all the time.

BRIDGET. I don't know what "all the time" means —

MICHAEL. *Bridget* —

BRIDGET. I do — I did — go there, yes.

MICHAEL. *When?*

BRIDGET. At night. Sometimes once a week, sometimes more. It depended.

MICHAEL. On what?

BRIDGET. On when they could meet. *(This throws Michael for a loop.)* It's where we met sometimes. They liked it because it was dark; they felt comfortable there.

MICHAEL. In the — the bar?

BRIDGET. Or around it, walking along the highway, under the stars. Different places, but always near there.

MICHAEL. Did the waitress — would she have known that they were — were — ?

BRIDGET. Oh, no. To her, they looked like regular, everyday people. Truckers, businessmen …

MICHAEL. Jesus Christ, how stupid do you think I am? How — fucking gullible?

BRIDGET. Not — *(Shakes her head.)* — I don't think that at —

MICHAEL. You met them at a bar — *(Biting down on his anger, barely.)* — can you at least *acknowledge* how absurd that sounds?

BRIDGET. It's the truth, Michael.

MICHAEL. Okay, well, forget the bar, forget sitting at the bar with these — these *things* —

BRIDGET. But I *did* —

MICHAEL. — and did you sit in their *trucks* with them? Because that's what people are telling me. Egan, the waitress. That you left with the men — the — the things — and that you went with them to their trucks — and to motels, a motel nearby. *(Beat.)* So are you saying that some of them *rent* motel rooms? That some of them *drive* trucks?

BRIDGET. We walked *by* trucks parked in the lot, we walked *by* a motel. If she saw anything, *that's* what she saw —

MICHAEL. She saw more, she saw more …

BRIDGET. What, did she follow me?

MICHAEL. Maybe —

BRIDGET. Maybe? Either she did or she didn't. What exactly did she say to you?

MICHAEL. Not to me, to —

BRIDGET. *(Incredulous.)* Wait, you *haven't* talked to her? *(Beat.)* You're accusing me of — of what, Michael? What are you accusing me of — *again?* (When you haven't even —)

MICHAEL. It's not just her, it's also — *(He shakes his head in anguish.)* I don't know you, I don't know you anymore … *(Bridget takes a step towards him —)*

BRIDGET. Michael —

MICHAEL. I've been reading your books, the ones Jeremy found upstairs. *(He shakes his head clear.)* And things *I* found, too, on the internet —

BRIDGET. Oh, well, of course.

MICHAEL. About abductions. About how sometimes it *does* happen like in the movies. They — they — they come in through the window, in the dead of night, riding beams of light, and they — they snatch people out of bed.

BRIDGET. As fast as you blow out a candle, they're gone, I know.

MICHAEL. But sometimes — sometimes — abductions *don't* happen that way. Sometimes, they *lure* us away — they trick us — fool us. And it doesn't happen suddenly, it happens slowly, over days, and they're — they're *cruel* about it. They play with us … they manipulate us … *then* they take us.

BRIDGET. That's why I've been saying — Why I need you to tell me — when Jeremy and I leave — I need you to tell me that you'll be with us. Because, Michael, listen to me: They *are* coming.

MICHAEL. You could do that? You could just leave me — leave the house — leave our *life* here?

BRIDGET. *It's what we have to do* — Not because it's what I want, or what Jeremy wants, but because we don't have a *choice* —

MICHAEL. I do, I could stay —

BRIDGET. *No, I've told you:* If you're here when they arrive, and they don't find what they're looking for … they'll *hurt* you. Or — or *worse* than hurt you. *(Michael considers this. Then:)*

MICHAEL. Tomorrow … I want you to take me to the bar — where you met them. I want to go. And the field, the cornfield, where they want Jeremy to wait.

BRIDGET. *Why?*

MICHAEL. Because — Bridget — you're my wife, aren't you?

BRIDGET. I — *(Gives up.)* — yes.

MICHAEL. I want to see what you've been doing, what you've been planning with them. *(Beat.)* I want to believe you. *(The lights fade to black. When they come up again, it's the next day. The living room is empty. Then we hear: a knock at the front door. Silence, then more knocking, and more. Until — Jeremy comes bounding down the stairs, carrying a suitcase. As soon as he hits the landing, the suitcase accidentally pops open, spilling a load of comic books to the floor.)*

JEREMY. Shit. *(Jeremy bends down to gather the comic books — hears more knocking — then continues to the door. As he nears it, he asks:)* Who is it? *(Jeremy opens the door; Egan strides in.)* Oh — hey. My mom and dad aren't home, it's just me, but — uhm, I *guess* you can come in if you want …

EGAN. *(As he comes in.)* You didn't wait for me to answer.

JEREMY. What?

EGAN. When you asked me who it was, when I was outside. I could've been anyone.

JEREMY. Oh, well, I mean — I wasn't worried.

EGAN. My son's the same way, my boy. He's also sixteen — Matthew, in your class, you know him — he also believes nothing bad'll ever happen to him. That's he's invincible, that he's gonna live forever, like a, like some — *(Beat.)* I try to tell him that the universe is a whole lot less benevolent than he supposes, and that sometimes, horrific things happen for no reason whatsoever, but do you think he listens? *(Egan is further into the living room, walking around.)*

JEREMY. Uhm — I'm sorry, but did you, like, *want* something?

EGAN. Your mom and dad — they're both out?

JEREMY. Yeah.

EGAN. Together?

JEREMY. Yeah.

38

EGAN. Really?

JEREMY. Yeah, they are, like, *married,* Sheriff. *(Egan stops at the pile of comic books, stoops to pick some up.)*

EGAN. These yours?

JEREMY. Yeah. Uhm —

EGAN. Matt reads them, too, he used to. Had boxes of them. Me, I collected baseball cards. I had a 1956 Hank Aaron, but my mother pitched it into the trash, God bless her, though I suppose — I guess we all have one of those stories. *(Looks up.)* You going on a trip?

JEREMY. What?

EGAN. The suitcase. You going on a trip?

JEREMY. No, that's just for — I'm just — *(Beat.)* Did you — uhm — want me to give my dad a message, Sheriff? Or something?

EGAN. If you don't mind. Your father and I had a ... funny talk, last time I was here. He asked me if I believed in aliens. *(Short pause as Egan tries to gauge Jeremy's reaction. Jeremy doesn't have one.)*

JEREMY. Yeah, okay, and?

EGAN. Well ... I didn't give him an answer.

JEREMY. Well, I mean ... I'm sure it's *fine,* Sheriff.

EGAN. Do you?

JEREMY. What, believe in aliens?

EGAN. Start there, sure. Your father says they can turn into anything, become anybody they want, you believe that? He called them ... uhm ...

JEREMY. ... shape-shifters. *(Jeremy is looking at Egan. The whole temperature in the room changes. Jeremy inches away from Egan nervously.)*

EGAN. Which sounds ... pretty far-fetched, if you ask me.

JEREMY. Sheriff ... maybe —

EGAN. How 'bout your mother's story, you believe that?

JEREMY. Uhm — which story would that be, Sheriff?

EGAN. The one your father didn't want me to hear, the one about aliens coming to take you away.

JEREMY. He — my dad told you that? (Jesus, he fucking told you that — that —)

EGAN. Because he wants me to stop it from happening. Because he wants my help.

JEREMY. Well, I mean — don't, like, worry, because they're *not* taking me away.

EGAN. It's also your mother he's concerned about. He thinks she might be … harmful to you.

JEREMY. My dad said that?

EGAN. He's afraid your mother's going to try and take you away from him. He wants my help to stop that from happening, too. If that's the case.

JEREMY. He wants you to keep me here?

EGAN. Yes.

JEREMY. Even though he knows …

EGAN. What, son? What does he know? *(But Jeremy is silent.)* Should I believe your father? Should I try to help him? *(Short pause, as Jeremy realizes something.)*

JEREMY. Oh, my God. You want me to, like, *corroborate* his story. To help you decide what to do. (God, why is everyone over the age of twenty so, like, transparent?)

EGAN. That's not what I'm —

JEREMY. If I say my dad's telling the truth, what — what do *you* do, Sheriff? Do you really try to — to "stop" my mom? By using — what, like, "force"?

EGAN. Of course not.

JEREMY. The thing you should know about my dad, Sheriff, since you're so *concerned* about us — is that my dad? He lies, okay? He — twists things around. Whatever he told you, he's lying about this. I mean, the truth is — the fact of the matter is — you have no idea who my dad really is, Sheriff — okay? — what he's really like — you don't know *anything*.

EGAN. I know enough.

JEREMY. Do you know why we moved here?

EGAN. Because your mother —

JEREMY. Because he hit her, Sheriff. Because he punched her and put her in the hospital.

EGAN. I — *(This has caught Egan by surprise.)* He doesn't think you know.

JEREMY. Yeah, which is — My Dad 101. *(Continuing quickly.)* After he'd done it, we were sitting in the hospital's cafeteria, and I asked him what happened. And he fabricated this story. Some — fairy tale. And the worst part? What's so pathetic? Is that I think he even *knew* I knew — that he was lying. Which is, like, *horrible.* But hey, that's my dad.

EGAN. I'm sorry.

JEREMY. Later, I asked my mom, and *she* confessed the truth. But then she told me to never talk about it again. "Because it'll be easier to live that way," she said, "And because, after awhile, it will be like it never happened." And I thought that was, like, the *saddest* thing I'd ever heard. *(Beat.)* But after awhile, it *was* like he'd never hit her. Because — I guess — if you pretend something long enough, it sometimes becomes true.

EGAN. Do you feel you're in danger here? From either your mother or your father? You feel threatened in any way?

JEREMY. I'm — *(Shaking his head "no.")* — fine, it's fine.

EGAN. I can't put you in protective custody unless you —

JEREMY. — yeah, I'd tell you if I *did* feel that way, all threatened like, but I don't, Sheriff, and right now, I gotta finish some stuff, but I'll tell my parents you came by, okay? *(Jeremy goes to the front door, holds it open.)*

EGAN. — all right. *(Egan starts to leave; before he actually makes it out, though, Jeremy asks him:)*

JEREMY. What should I say your answer was — about the aliens? *(A beat, then:)*

EGAN. That I don't believe they exist. *(With that, Egan exits, Jeremy shuts the door, and the lights fade. Lights up. It is later that afternoon. The living room is empty. After a few moments, Michael and Bridget enter. Michael is shaken. He sits down on the couch. Bridget hovers in the room, unsure, then —)*

BRIDGET. I'm sorry there wasn't anything. Whatever you were looking for? Michael? Imprints in the grass, a scorched patch of…? *(More carefully here.)* And nothing at the bar, either.

MICHAEL. Jesus. To imagine that my wife would ever go there to — to —

BRIDGET. I wish — I *wanted* her to be there. That woman who told you those lies. *(Beat.)* I wanted her to say them in front me — *to* me.

MICHAEL. Going to those places with you. The field and … *(His voice trails off.)*

BRIDGET. What, Michael?

MICHAEL. I *felt* … I *sensed* … Everywhere …

BRIDGET. Yes. *(Nodding.)* That's right.

MICHAEL. An otherness … Completely … unfamiliar …

BRIDGET. That's them. That's … vestiges they leave behind. Traces.

MICHAEL. Of…?

BRIDGET. Themselves. Where they come from. What they can do.

MICHAEL. *(To himself.)* Anything … *(To her.)* Is that right? They can do anything?

BRIDGET. You — you understand now? What's at stake?

MICHAEL. I'm trying, I'm trying to …

BRIDGET. No, you *have* to, Michael. Now, right now. You've had long enough — too long —

MICHAEL. Bridget, you're not — *(Mini-beat.)* This isn't all because you're trying to trick me?

BRIDGET. What? Of course not. Why would I be — ?

MICHAEL. Not you — not Bridget — *(Jeremy comes bounding down the stairs, into the living room, between his mom and dad.)*

JEREMY. What's … what's going on? *(Silence from them. They are focused on each other.)*

BRIDGET. You asked me to go to those places, I went. You wanted me to try and meet this woman, I agreed. I'm not — No one's *hiding* anything from you —

MICHAEL. — all right — *(Mini-beat.)* — all right. *(Things hang in the air a bit. Bridget and Jeremy are unsure what it means, but hopeful.)*

JEREMY. "All right" meaning … you'll come with us?

MICHAEL. Yes …

BRIDGET. Thank you —

JEREMY. So we can go? Right this second?

BRIDGET. No, it's almost night now. We'd have to make most of the trip in the dark, which means they could … *(Beat.)* They could be watching us, watching the house, right now.

JEREMY. *(To himself.)* Jesus, I hate that, I really, *really* hate that … *(Michael is looking at his wife.)*

BRIDGET. We'll leave tomorrow, as planned, as soon as the sun comes up — *(Bridget leads Jeremy off, up the stairs. After they've exited, Michael walks to the bottom of the stairs, looks up after them. He is looking at them as the lights slowly fade. Lights up. The next day. Bridget is coming into the living room from outside. Michael is sitting at the window, looking outside at the dawning day.)*

MICHAEL. It must've been dark still, when you left, before dawn. (Was it?) It was when *I* woke up, and your side of the bed wasn't even *warm*. *(Mini-beat.)* Where were you — where did you go?

BRIDGET. I, I had to meet with them one last time to, to confirm everything for today — tonight, I mean. So they wouldn't suspect

anything. *(She can tell something's wrong with him.)* Michael …
(Michael turns to Bridget, fixes her with a stare.)

MICHAEL. When you weren't here again, this morning …

BRIDGET. I just told you —

MICHAEL. … I thought: "Enough. You've waited — You protect
Jeremy yourself from whatever's coming — what's already here."

BRIDGET. That's what we're doing, that's why we're going —

MICHAEL. He's already gone — I sent Jeremy away.

BRIDGET. What? Why?

MICHAEL. To protect him. *(Fighting panic, Bridget starts calling
for her son:)*

BRIDGET. Jeremy? *JEREMY?*

MICHAEL. He's not here —

BRIDGET. WHERE, Michael — *WHERE* is he?

MICHAEL. Safe from you.

BRIDGET. From…? *(Unsaid: "me.")*

MICHAEL. You — convinced me. I believe you now, I believe *in*
you now. I'm looking at you, what you are, what you *really* are …
(He can't say it, though. And Bridget moves closer to him.)

BRIDGET. What, Michael? What am I? *(She reaches out to touch
him.)* What do you think I — ?

MICHAEL. *DON'T* — *(Mini-beat.)* — don't touch me —
(Bridget pulls back, looks at Michael.) How long would it last — if
I went along with you — if I went away with you? How long
would you stay with me? How long would it be before you and
Jeremy just — vanished one night?

BRIDGET. Never. Michael —

MICHAEL. You look — so much like her. I want — so badly —
for you to *be* her.

BRIDGET. Who?

MICHAEL. It would be so easy to accept you and not the truth,
but I can't, I can't do it. (God …)

BRIDGET. What are you talking about?

MICHAEL. Please stop using her voice. You sound so much like
her, I can't — *bear* it!

BRIDGET. "Sound so much like" — ?

MICHAEL. MY WIFE —

BRIDGET. Michael —

MICHAEL. — *I don't think you're my wife! (And there it is. And
Bridget finally accepts that Michael has really lost it.)* If she's dead, tell

43

me. If you've taken her someplace else because she doesn't want to be with me —

BRIDGET. *LOOK AT ME, MICHAEL! (She holds her arms open.)* I'm Bridget. I'm your wife. You love me.

MICHAEL. No.

BRIDGET. Yes. *(Bridget's mind starts racing.)* You're not making any sense. How could I not be Bridget, look at me.

MICHAEL. *That's what I've been doing* — and — and … *(He shakes his head.)* What exists between people, what binds them together …

BRIDGET. Look at me — what are you saying?

MICHAEL. The first night Bridget and I spent together was after a football game, a college football game in late November, right before Thanksgiving. It started to rain, and we ran to my apartment — we were sopping wet — we were freezing — and we just — we held each other, under my blankets, all of them piled on top of us — until we were warm again. *(Beat.)* You could tell me about that, about everything that happened, but you can't make me feel it — that same warmth. Bridget could. All I had to do was *look* at her, and I'd start to feel warm again.

BRIDGET. You're not right, this isn't — *(Mini-beat.)* Can't you tell what's happening? You're trying to make sense of everything around you and you're — you're shutting down. If you would just stop — and think clearly for five minutes — you would realize how crazy this is — how crazy you're being. *(Mini-beat.)* I'm your wife, I'm Bridget. Ask me something only Bridget — only *I* would know. Ask me something, go ahead. *(This next exchange happens fast, lines overlapping.)*

MICHAEL. Memories can be stolen —

BRIDGET. Ask me what your favorite color is.

MICHAEL. — they can be absorbed —

BRIDGET. Orange. Ask me what I ate every day when I was pregnant.

MICHAEL. — you could've researched Bridget the same way she —

BRIDGET. Fried chicken. Ask me what I gave you for Christmas last year.

MICHAEL. — this doesn't prove anything, you're not convincing —

BRIDGET. A printer — which took you *months* to install —

MICHAEL. — just because you know a few random facts —

BRIDGET. *These are not random facts, Michael, these are our lives!*

Our life. Together. We *love* each other. *Ask me* —
MICHAEL. We don't have a life together, we don't have any —
BRIDGET. *Ask me what I thought — how it felt — when you hit me, Michael! (Pause.)*
MICHAEL. Don't. You can't —
BRIDGET. Ask me —
MICHAEL. I'm not — I won't —
BRIDGET. Ask me what it tasted like, the blood from my broken nose that went into my mouth. Like a penny. Ask me how it was, having to explain to everyone who asked me about it, the bruises. And I don't just mean our son, my mom and dad, my sister — I mean the rest of the world. Ask me — ask me how terrified I was right before and right after it happened. Thinking that everything I knew about you, everything I knew about the kind of person you were, was wrong. Ask me how it felt when you came to the hospital, crying, and grabbed my hand, and begged me to forgive you, to not leave you. "Believe me," you said, "this will *never* happen again. I will *never* do that — to you — again. You have no reason to, Bridget, but believe me, believe *in* me." You said. And I did. I believed in you. Now — now you believe in *me*, Michael, in what I'm telling you. I *am* your wife. I *do* love you. Whatever you're seeing, and thinking, and thinking you're seeing, hold onto those two things. I *am* Bridget. I *do* love you. And — and something truly *horrible* will happen to Jeremy if we don't leave with him today. Believe in *that*, Michael.
MICHAEL. I … (*Bridget opens her arms wide, stands there for a few moments. Without warning, Michael rushes Bridget and hugs her tightly. After a few moments, he starts sobbing. Bridget hugs him back. They hug and hug. Michael is overcome.*) Oh, God … Oh — God …
BRIDGET. Do you feel that? Do you feel me?
MICHAEL. You're — warm …
BRIDGET. Yes. Yes, Michael. (*They are still in the embrace.*) You believe who I am now? That I'm —
MICHAEL. I can't …
BRIDGET. You *can*. Believe that only we can keep Jeremy safe.
MICHAEL. I want …
BRIDGET. And that once it's over, once this has passed, we'll be as happy as we were. There won't be anything bad between us anymore. Nothing but us — and Jeremy — and starting over. You want that, don't you?

MICHAEL. Yes.

BRIDGET. Then do this for me. For Jeremy. Tell me where he is.

MICHAEL. *E ... Egan has him ...*

BRIDGET. Has Jeremy?

MICHAEL. He's hiding him ... I don't know where. Not at his house and not at the station, so we can't —

BRIDGET. Michael —

MICHAEL. They left while you were out doing — getting ready —

BRIDGET. You just — you handed him over to — ?

MICHAEL. Egan knows what's at stake. He'll keep Jeremy away from the house. Until tomorrow morning, when —

BRIDGET. But you don't even know who that man is, that — sheriff. He's a — he's a *stranger* —

MICHAEL. Egan's a good man —

BRIDGET. Can we — is there a number to call him?

MICHAEL. No, he won't — I told him that if we tried, he shouldn't —

BRIDGET. *(Panic.)* MICHAEL —

MICHAEL. He'll keep Jeremy safe —

BRIDGET. No, but what if he can't? What if they find Jeremy wherever he is? Or if they don't leave — if they wait for him?

MICHAEL. That — You said — They only had a small window —

BRIDGET. I *think* — They *said* — But ... *(The horror of the situation:)* Oh, God, Michael, you don't know, you don't know ... *(Unsaid: "what you've done ... ")*

MICHAEL. Tomorrow morning, Egan will come here with Jeremy, and —

BRIDGET. *You don't know that, Michael, you don't know THEM — (And then it dawns on Michael ... he doesn't.)* But you will ... You will ... *(And very slowly, Bridget goes to the couch and sits down, next to Michael. She is trying not to shake, not to cry. She puts her hand in Michael's and the two of them sit there, waiting, waiting ... as the lights outside the window change from morning, to afternoon, to dusk, to complete black — and a spot comes up on Jeremy, surrounded by darkness. He speaks to the audience:)*

JEREMY. That's how I imagine them: sitting side by side, holding hands like little kids, waiting for ... what? For something that's ... unknowable, I think. *(Beat.)* I say "imagine" because I don't know what my mom and dad experienced that day, that night. If They came down from the skies and spared my parents ... Or if They passed over our house without making themselves known … Or … anything. *(Beat.)* And my mom and dad … I don't think they ever find out what happens to me. If anything, they hear Egan's story — that the plan was for us to spend the night in a motel, just out of town, but I got away from him — snuck away, slipped away somehow — and they spend their lives wondering:

Did I run away…?

Is Egan lying because *he* did something to me?

Or was I…? *(Short pause.)* My mom once told me that stars are celestial bodies which radiate light from within … *(Beat.)* I picture her so clearly sometimes, at night, standing in front of our house, looking up, wondering: "Is that what he is now? A star? Shining down on me — on everyone — forever? Far above us, burning away in the dark…?" *(Slow blackout as the stage fills with stars.)*

End of Play

PROPERTY LIST

Answering machine
Milk, 2 bowls of cereal, spoons
List
Jacket
Phone
Stack of journals, scrapbooks with clippings
Stack of books
Apron, plate of eggs
Suitcase filled with comic books

SOUND EFFECTS

Answering machine beep, messages
Night sounds: crickets, wind
Phone ring

NEW PLAYS

★ **GUARDIANS by Peter Morris.** In this unflinching look at war, a disgraced American soldier discloses the truth about Abu Ghraib prison, and a clever English journalist reveals how he faked a similar story for the London tabloids. "Compelling, sympathetic and powerful." *–NY Times.* "Sends you into a state of moral turbulence." *–Sunday Times (UK).* "Nothing short of remarkable." *–Village Voice.* [1M, 1W] ISBN: 978-0-8222-2177-7

★ **BLUE DOOR by Tanya Barfield.** Three generations of men (all played by one actor), from slavery through Black Power, challenge Lewis, a tenured professor of mathematics, to embark on a journey combining past and present. "A teasing flare for words." *–Village Voice.* "Unfailingly thought-provoking." *–LA Times.* "The play moves with the speed and logic of a dream." *–Seattle Weekly.* [2M] ISBN: 978-0-8222-2209-5

★ **THE INTELLIGENT DESIGN OF JENNY CHOW by Rolin Jones.** This irreverent "techno-comedy" chronicles one brilliant woman's quest to determine her heritage and face her fears with the help of her astounding creation called Jenny Chow. "Boldly imagined." *–NY Times.* "Fantastical and funny." *–Variety.* "Harvests many laughs and finally a few tears." *–LA Times.* [3M, 3W] ISBN: 978-0-8222-2071-8

★ **SOUVENIR by Stephen Temperley.** Florence Foster Jenkins, a wealthy society eccentric, suffers under the delusion that she is a great coloratura soprano—when in fact the opposite is true. "Hilarious and deeply touching. Incredibly moving and breathtaking." *–NY Daily News.* "A sweet love letter of a play." *–NY Times.* "Wildly funny. Completely charming." *–Star-Ledger.* [1M, 1W] ISBN: 978-0-8222-2157-9

★ **ICE GLEN by Joan Ackermann.** In this touching period comedy, a beautiful poetess dwells in idyllic obscurity on a Berkshire estate with a band of unlikely cohorts. "A beautifully written story of nature and change." *–Talkin' Broadway.* "A lovely play which will leave you with a lot to think about." *–CurtainUp.* "Funny, moving and witty." *–Metroland (Boston).* [4M, 3W] ISBN: 978-0-8222-2175-3

★ **THE LAST DAYS OF JUDAS ISCARIOT by Stephen Adly Guirgis.** Set in a time-bending, darkly comic world between heaven and hell, this play reexamines the plight and fate of the New Testament's most infamous sinner. "An unforced eloquence that finds the poetry in lowdown street talk." *–NY Times.* "A real jaw-dropper." *–Variety.* "An extraordinary play." *–Guardian (UK).* [10M, 5W] ISBN: 978-0-8222-2082-4

DRAMATISTS PLAY SERVICE, INC.
440 Park Avenue South, New York, NY 10016 212-683-8960 Fax 212-213-1539
postmaster@dramatists.com   www.dramatists.com

NEW PLAYS

★ **THE GREAT AMERICAN TRAILER PARK MUSICAL music and lyrics by David Nehls, book by Betsy Kelso.** Pippi, a stripper on the run, has just moved into Armadillo Acres, wreaking havoc among the tenants of Florida's most exclusive trailer park. "Adultery, strippers, murderous ex-boyfriends, Costco and the Ice Capades. Undeniable fun." *–NY Post.* "Joyful and unashamedly vulgar." *–The New Yorker.* "Sparkles with treasure." *–New York Sun.* [2M, 5W] ISBN: 978-0-8222-2137-1

★ **MATCH by Stephen Belber.** When a young Seattle couple meet a prominent New York choreographer, they are led on a fraught journey that will change their lives forever. "Uproariously funny, deeply moving, enthralling theatre." *–NY Daily News.* "Prolific laughs and ear-to-ear smiles." *–NY Magazine.* [2M, 1W] ISBN: 978-0-8222-2020-6

★ **MR. MARMALADE by Noah Haidle.** Four-year-old Lucy's imaginary friend, Mr. Marmalade, doesn't have much time for her—not to mention he has a cocaine addiction and a penchant for pornography. "Alternately hilarious and heartbreaking." *–The New Yorker.* "A mature and accomplished play." *–LA Times.* "Scathingly observant comedy." *–Miami Herald.* [4M, 2W] ISBN: 978-0-8222-2142-5

★ **MOONLIGHT AND MAGNOLIAS by Ron Hutchinson.** Three men cloister themselves as they work tirelessly to reshape a screenplay that's just not working—*Gone with the Wind.* "Consumers of vintage Hollywood insider stories will eat up Hutchinson's diverting conjecture." *–Variety.* "A lot of fun." *–NY Post.* "A Hollywood dream-factory farce." *–Chicago Sun-Times.* [3M, 1W] ISBN: 978-0-8222-2084-8

★ **THE LEARNED LADIES OF PARK AVENUE by David Grimm, translated and freely adapted from Molière's *Les Femmes Savantes*.** Dicky wants to marry Betty, but her mother's plan is for Betty to wed a most pompous man. "A brave, brainy and barmy revision." *–Hartford Courant.* "A rare but welcome bird in contemporary theatre." *–New Haven Register.* "Roll over Cole Porter." *–Boston Globe.* [5M, 5W] ISBN: 978-0-8222-2135-7

★ **REGRETS ONLY by Paul Rudnick.** A sparkling comedy of Manhattan manners that explores the latest topics in marriage, friendships and squandered riches. "One of the funniest quip-meisters on the planet." *–NY Times.* "Precious moments of hilarity. Devastatingly accurate political and social satire." *–BackStage.* "Great fun." *–CurtainUp.* [3M, 3W] ISBN: 978-0-8222-2223-1

DRAMATISTS PLAY SERVICE, INC.
440 Park Avenue South, New York, NY 10016 212-683-8960 Fax 212-213-1539
postmaster@dramatists.com www.dramatists.com

NEW PLAYS

★ **AFTER ASHLEY by Gina Gionfriddo.** A teenager is unwillingly thrust into the national spotlight when a family tragedy becomes talk-show fodder. "A work that virtually any audience would find accessible." –*NY Times.* "Deft characterization and caustic humor." –*NY Sun.* "A smart satirical drama." –*Variety.* [4M, 2W] ISBN: 978-0-8222-2099-2

★ **THE RUBY SUNRISE by Rinne Groff.** Twenty-five years after Ruby struggles to realize her dream of inventing the first television, her daughter faces similar battles of faith as she works to get Ruby's story told on network TV. "Measured and intelligent, optimistic yet clear-eyed." –*NY Magazine.* "Maintains an exciting sense of ingenuity." –*Village Voice.* "Sinuous theatrical flair." –*Broadway.com.* [3M, 4W] ISBN: 978-0-8222-2140-1

★ **MY NAME IS RACHEL CORRIE taken from the writings of Rachel Corrie, edited by Alan Rickman and Katharine Viner.** This solo piece tells the story of Rachel Corrie who was killed in Gaza by an Israeli bulldozer set to demolish a Palestinian home. "Heartbreaking urgency. An invigoratingly detailed portrait of a passionate idealist." –*NY Times.* "Deeply authentically human." –*USA Today.* "A stunning dramatization." –*CurtainUp.* [1W] ISBN: 978-0-8222-2222-4

★ **ALMOST, MAINE by John Cariani.** This charming midwinter night's dream of a play turns romantic clichés on their ear as it chronicles the painfully hilarious amorous adventures (and misadventures) of residents of a remote northern town that doesn't quite exist. "A whimsical approach to the joys and perils of romance." –*NY Times.* "Sweet, poignant and witty." –*NY Daily News.* "Aims for the heart by way of the funny bone." –*Star-Ledger.* [2M, 2W] ISBN: 978-0-8222-2156-2

★ **Mitch Albom's TUESDAYS WITH MORRIE by Jeffrey Hatcher and Mitch Albom, based on the book by Mitch Albom.** The true story of Brandeis University professor Morrie Schwartz and his relationship with his student Mitch Albom. "A touching, life-affirming, deeply emotional drama." –*NY Daily News.* "You'll laugh. You'll cry." –*Variety.* "Moving and powerful." –*NY Post.* [2M] ISBN: 978-0-8222-2188-3

★ **DOG SEES GOD: CONFESSIONS OF A TEENAGE BLOCKHEAD by Bert V. Royal.** An abused pianist and a pyromaniac ex-girlfriend contribute to the teen-angst of America's most hapless kid. "A welcome antidote to the notion that the *Peanuts* gang provides merely American cuteness." –*NY Times.* "Hysterically funny." –*NY Post.* "The *Peanuts* kids have finally come out of their shells." –*Time Out.* [4M, 4W] ISBN: 978-0-8222-2152-4

DRAMATISTS PLAY SERVICE, INC.
440 Park Avenue South, New York, NY 10016 212-683-8960 Fax 212-213-1539
postmaster@dramatists.com www.dramatists.com

NEW PLAYS

★ **RABBIT HOLE by David Lindsay-Abaire.** Winner of the 2007 Pulitzer Prize. Becca and Howie Corbett have everything a couple could want until a life-shattering accident turns their world upside down. "An intensely emotional examination of grief, laced with wit." *–Variety.* "A transcendent and deeply affecting new play." *–Entertainment Weekly.* "Painstakingly beautiful." *–BackStage.* [2M, 3W] ISBN: 978-0-8222-2154-8

★ **DOUBT, A Parable by John Patrick Shanley.** Winner of the 2005 Pulitzer Prize and Tony Award. Sister Aloysius, a Bronx school principal, takes matters into her own hands when she suspects the young Father Flynn of improper relations with one of the male students. "All the elements come invigoratingly together like clockwork." *–Variety.* "Passionate, exquisite, important, engrossing." *–NY Newsday.* [1M, 3W] ISBN: 978-0-8222-2219-4

★ **THE PILLOWMAN by Martin McDonagh.** In an unnamed totalitarian state, an author of horrific children's stories discovers that someone has been making his stories come true. "A blindingly bright black comedy." *–NY Times.* "McDonagh's least forgiving, bravest play." *–Variety.* "Thoroughly startling and genuinely intimidating." *–Chicago Tribune.* [4M, 5 bit parts (2M, 1W, 1 boy, 1 girl)] ISBN: 978-0-8222-2100-5

★ **GREY GARDENS book by Doug Wright, music by Scott Frankel, lyrics by Michael Korie.** The hilarious and heartbreaking story of Big Edie and Little Edie Bouvier Beale, the eccentric aunt and cousin of Jacqueline Kennedy Onassis, once bright names on the social register who became East Hampton's most notorious recluses. "An experience no passionate theatergoer should miss." *–NY Times.* "A unique and unmissable musical." *–Rolling Stone.* [4M, 3W, 2 girls] ISBN: 978-0-8222-2181-4

★ **THE LITTLE DOG LAUGHED by Douglas Carter Beane.** Mitchell Green could make it big as the hot new leading man in Hollywood if Diane, his agent, could just keep him in the closet. "Devastatingly funny." *–NY Times.* "An out-and-out delight." *–NY Daily News.* "Full of wit and wisdom." *–NY Post.* [2M, 2W] ISBN: 978-0-8222-2226-2

★ **SHINING CITY by Conor McPherson.** A guilt-ridden man reaches out to a therapist after seeing the ghost of his recently deceased wife. "Haunting, inspired and glorious." *–NY Times.* "Simply breathtaking and astonishing." *–Time Out.* "A thoughtful, artful, absorbing new drama." *–Star-Ledger.* [3M, 1W] ISBN: 978-0-8222-2187-6

DRAMATISTS PLAY SERVICE, INC.
440 Park Avenue South, New York, NY 10016 212-683-8960 Fax 212-213-1539
postmaster@dramatists.com www.dramatists.com